First published 2000 AD
This edition © Wooden Books 2001 AD

Published by Wooden Books Ltd.
Walkmill, Cascob, Presteigne, Powys, Wales LD8 2NT

British Library Cataloguing in Publication Data
Heath, R.
Stonehenge

A CIP catalogue record for this weighty book
is available from the British Library

ISBN 1 902418 25 5

Printed and bound in Great Britain
by The Cromwell Press,
Trowbridge, Wiltshire, UK.

STONEHENGE

STONHING

by

Robin Heath

To Rebecca, Lea and Matthew.

Pictures have been taken from a wide selection of rare antiquarian books
and are mostly credited where they appear. The illustration on the cover
and below is by Lucas De Herre, from 1575, the plans on the following
page show various interpretations of Stonehenge, the engravings on page 3
are from Inigo Jones' book of 1655, the top picture on page 25 is from
Walpoole's late 18th century 'Modern British Traveller', illustrations
on pages 27 and 54 courtesy of Eoghan MacColl,
other illustrations are by the author.

The earliest drawing of Stonehenge

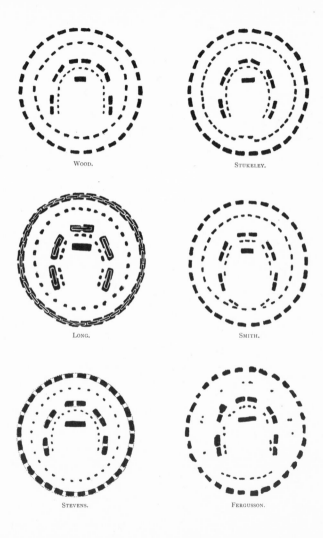

WOOD.

STUKELEY.

LONG.

SMITH.

STEVENS.

FERGUSSON.

INTRODUCTION

Stonehenge is Britain's national temple. As for all temples built by man, Stonehenge has solid foundations in the earth whilst its huge stones aspire upwards to the heavens. In contemplating this temple, within the landscape and skyscape it has reflected for over five millenia, we see into the mind of the architects and are connected back to our ancestors. We also glimpse something of their spiritual values, which are timeless.

Archaeologists still do not yet know why Stonehenge was built, nor its purpose. These big questions remain un-answered, and into the resulting vacuum flows speculation, theory and rumour. Stonehenge thus remains enigmatic, tenaciously holding onto its secrets and mysteries, whilst we humans come and go in a relative flash.

This little book illustrates the re-emergence of Stonehenge into the collective modern psyche. Following an incredible 1500 years of constructional evolution, Stonehenge fell into disuse around 1500 BC, and was not re-discovered in our era until about 1500 AD. The hideously-named 'Car Park Postholes' may even date back 8000 years, to 6000 BC.

Stonehenge is far more than just an impressive array of huge stones. If it were merely that then one must ask why today it invokes so much fuss, timed, to chronological perfection, each and every midsummer solstice, more than five millenia after the ditch was first dug. Stonehenge has become a symbol or icon of *Albion*, of the ancient wisdom of Britain, and of different cultural values from a lost time. That is why it still maintains a power and a presence to which we respond - we still dance at Stonehenge to the cosmic rhythms, most obviously those of the solstitial Sun.

As we enter a new millenium, Stonehenge's sixth, the apparently disparate subjects of archaeology, astronomy, metrology, sacred geometry and even shamanism are slowly converging to reveal an holistic Megalithic Science.

Once part of an impressively large culture of stone circles, Stonehenge yet differs from all the rest. Unique, it stands within a neolithic cultural time-capsule, the remains of a once wealthy and evidently learned tribal community. Their legacy of stone is left for us to reckon with.

St Dogmaels, 2000 AD

DIGGING IN THE DARK
the rediscovery of Stonehenge

Ever since the end of the Dark Ages, descriptions and illustrations of Stonehenge have been interwoven with the cultural fantasies of the time. So remote is the culture which built the monument that we should not be surprised at this. The King's architect Inigo Jones added a sixth trilithon to link Stonehenge to Roman styles (*see page 45*), whilst Lucas De Herre's charming yet naïve sketch (*see cover*) is the first known illustration, drawn 'on the spot' in 1575.

The Age of the Antiquarian dawned around 1650 with John Aubrey, and later William Stukeley - Stonehenge now became *temple plus druids*. Exit Roman and Greek influences and enter *rude British*. The bizarre engraving opposite is from William Camden's *Britannia* of 1605.

Plundering became rife - that notorious duo, Colt-Hoare and Cunningham, practiced 'reverse alchemy' - replacing struck gold with lead tokens. Within the last century, Colonel Hawley and Professors Richard Atkinson and Alexander Thom pioneered more accurate surveying and dating of Stonehenge, but many mysteries remain.

A The Stones call'd Corfstones, 12 Tonn Wright
24 foot high, 7 broad, and 16 round
B The Stones call'd Coronets, of 6 or 7 Tonns
C The place where Mens bones are dug up

J. Kip.

5

THE SALISBURY LANDSCAPE
around Stonehenge

Stonehenge forms the centrepiece of a rich heritage – the remains of the Wessex Culture. Within a few miles the rambler may discover various types of barrow, two in-explicable cursusses, Woodhenge, a long 'avenue', many singleton stones and not a few large postholes. Local museums display wonderful treasures taken from the earth here.

The impressive Stonehenge cursus is over two miles long and averages 140 yards in width, enclosing over 100 acres of land. It has been variously described as a UFO runway, tornado strip or jousting arena. It was probably none of these, although speculation bids us to wonder why anyone might wish to construct such strange alignments, especially so near to Stonehenge itself (*see also page 10*).

Stonehenge appears curiously and not ideally sited within its landscape. Built on sloping ground, the perfectly level ring of lintels required supporting stones of differing heights. The bulk of these stones, weighing up to 50 tonnes, had to be transported over 20 miles. This eloquently informs even the casual visitor that the architect chose the location of the site with great forethought.

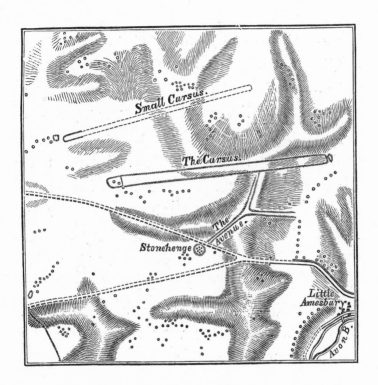

STONEHENGE CULTURE
the people who built Stonehenge

What little we know about the people that built Stonehenge comes from archaeology and radiocarbon dating. Some fine gold artefacts, polished maces, riveted sword-hafts and elegant pottery contrast with crude sarsen maul hammers, flint arrowheads, arthritic bones and low life-expectancy.

Polished mace and axe heads (*below*) date from about 2500 BC and are often made from semi-precious stones. Opposite left are examples of fine beaker-folk pottery (2300 BC). Opposite right can be seen a selection of finely knapped flint arrowheads, whilst a decorated ceremonial bronze axe-head from 2000 BC reveals a culture whose functional priorities were balanced with artistic expertise.

It is worthwhile imagining how one could equip, feed and organise the labourers who undertook the estimated twelve million man-hours it took to erect Stonehenge.

RIDDLES REMAIN
the cursus and the loony fringe

Archaeologists have labelled most alternative theories on Stonehenge as belonging to 'the loony fringe of dotty archaeology'. However, it was a dowser, Guy Underwood, who first correctly determined that Stonehenge was built in 2650 BC, when the orthodoxy dated it around 1750 BC. His map of the earth energies within Stonehenge is shown opposite. Stukeley's engraving of the cursus is shown below.

It was a retired engineer, Professor Thom, who discovered the unit of length used by the builders. In the 1960's renowned astronomers Professor Fred Hoyle and Dr Gerald Hawkins 'decoded' the astronomy of Stonehenge; hardly loony fringe, and it was the archaeologists who went dotty.

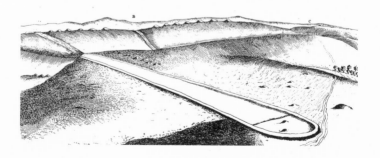

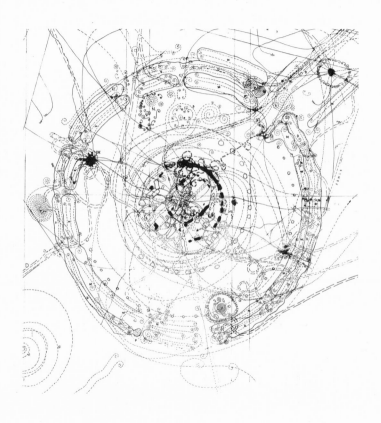

THE FIRST STONEHENGE
an implosion over 1500 years

Stonehenge's concentric circles of stones and postholes moved inwards with time – the very opposite of a raindrop falling on water. This implosion evolved over 1500 years.

The *outer ditch and bank,* once 6ft (2m) high, is dated to around 3150 BC. The axis entrance, flanked by the then upright *slaughter stone* and a long gone companion stone, was filled with many experimental posts, apparently to monitor the most northerly moonrises each month (*opposite centre*), particularly the extreme midwinter full moonrise which occurs every eighteen years and seven months.

The entrance was later widened and the angle changed to that of the midsummer sunrise. The *heelstone*, 'moated' within a small circular ditch, marked the start of an 1800 foot long *avenue*. Stonehenge apparently became less and less lunar and more and more a solar observatory.

The name 'heelstone' perhaps derives from the Welsh or Greek word for Sun, *haul* and *helios* respectively. Another name, 'Friar's Heel', is thought to refer to a footprint indented on the stone's surface, although *freos heol* is Celtic for "ascending Sun".

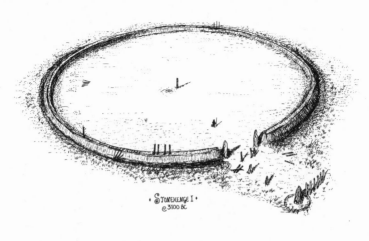

· STONEHENGE I ·
@ 3100 BC

MOST NORTHERLY MOONRISE

MIDSUMMER SUNRISE

13

AUBREY HOLES & STATION STONES
fifty-six and a five to twelve rectangle

Around 3000 BC, the circle of 56 Aubrey holes was dug, some think to provide sockets to house large posts supporting a wooden henge platform long since rotted away (*opposite top*).

Three centuries later, the four station stones were placed defining the corners of a 5:12 rectangle on the Aubrey perimeter, making its diagonal 13 'units' (*opposite lower left*), each of 8 Megalithic yards (MYs) in length. Thus the inside diameter of the Aubrey circle is 104 MY or 283ft (86.2m). A Megalithic yard is 2.72ft or 0.829m.

Two of the station stones (92 and 94) were erected each within a small circular ditch. They may have been twelve feet in height. Now vanished, the other two stones remain on site today, a nine foot recumbent and a four foot stub.

A central bluestone 'henge' existed around this time – several bluestones on the site possess mortises, tenons or tonguing. Stone 68 even has a grooved edge (*opposite bottom right and see page 43*). Perhaps thirty-eight pairs of bluestones were intended to complete a circle of radial trilithons just inside the Sarsen circle, apparently never completed.

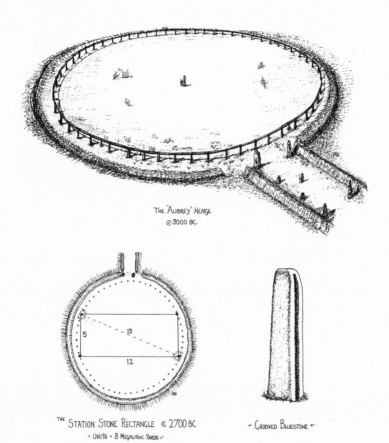

The "Aubrey" Henge
@ 3000 BC

THE STATION STONE RECTANGLE © 2700 BC
~ UNITS = 8 MEGALITHIC YARDS ~

5

13

12

~ Grooved Bluestone ~

SARSENS AND TRILITHONS
prehistoric monsters from a neolithic past

Around 2600 BC, the famous Sarsen circle we see today was constructed. Within it, probably at the same time, the five massive *trilithons* were also erected; three stand today. These monsters do not fit through the gaps in the sarsen circle – common sense dictates this sequence of construction.

The sarsens are dressed on their inner faces and rise about 13 feet above the ground, whilst the graded trilithons are more finely dressed and vary from 15 to 24 feet in height. The mean diameter of the sarsen circle is 100.8 feet, whereas the trilithons take up an ellipse shape 40 by 70 feet.

Inside both sarsen and trilithon constructions may be found the remnants of the earlier bluestone henge, dismantled and the stones later recycled, perhaps after 2000 BC, into a horseshoe of slender dressed stones 39 feet across, and a circle about 75 feet in diameter of undressed bluestones (*page 33*).

The Sarsen circle may be placed precisely from the earlier Aubrey circle using the geometry of a seven-pointed star (*shown opposite*). This is the more remarkable when we see true north and the midsummer sunrise separated by a seventh of a circle at the latitude of Stonehenge.

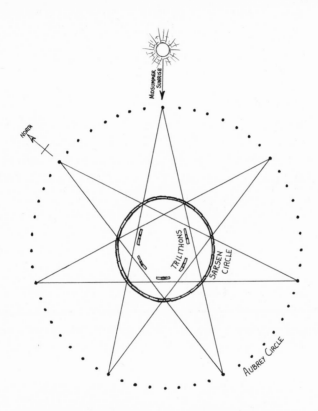

~ A SEVENFOLD GEOMETRY ~
THE SARSEN CIRCLE AND TRILITHONS
IN RELATIONSHIP TO THE AUBREY CIRCLE

MEAN SARSEN DIAMETER = 100.8 ft
MEAN AUBREY DIAMETER = 282.8 ft
RATIO ~ $\frac{7}{19}$

WOODWORK IN STONE
how to do joined up megaliths

Around the top of the thirty sarsen uprights was placed a perfectly level circle of thirty curved sarsen lintels. In order to fix these securely, some thirteen feet above the ground, each was tongued at one end and grooved at the other, like pieces of a jigsaw. In addition, each upright was dressed with two tenons which mated with corresponding mortises on the lintels. The visitor may observe the tenons on many sarsen uprights where the lintels have fallen. These jointing techniques derive from the wood joiner's craft.

The mighty trilithon uprights carried a large single tenon and their lintels were duly mortised. The tallest stone (56) still sports its tenon, like a boy's schoolcap thrown up as a prank, whilst its curiously double-mortised lintel has fallen.

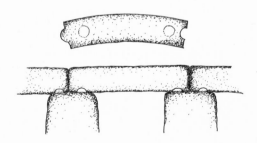

2000 BC - an idealised view from the south showing the half-width sarsen

1900 AD - Stonehenge before restoration showing a silhouetted bluestone (62)

1900 AD - view from the south showing the once perilously leaning trilithon upright (56)
Three pictures from Barclay's 'Stonehenge', 1895 (see also page 43).

19

THE MODERN PICTURE
what you see is what's left

The construction of Stonehenge began around 3150 BC and was over by about 1500 BC. Thenceforth, it fell victim to the vaguaries of the British climate and lay at the mercy of cultural change. As late as 1917 the authorities submitted an application to demolish Stonehenge as "a dangerous hazard to low-flying aircraft"! Remarkably, it has survived - after a fashion - the site is now enshrouded in security fences, a car park and souvenir palace, temples to a different god.

Many visitors have carved graffiti on the stones, which has conferred on them an *ersatz* immortality. Mycean daggers may be discerned. The relentless erosion of the sarsen stone by wind, rain and frost has produced some bizarre gnarling and pock-marks. In 1797 trilithon four fell, shaking the ground miles away. During the last night of the nineteenth century, a sarsen upright and its lintel fell (stones 22 & 122).

Some fallen stones have been 'restored', not always in their original positions. Others have disappeared off-site, perhaps to be broken up and used in less interesting buildings.

Opposite is a French re-engraving of two prints by David Loggan, who died in 1693.

Vûe de STONE-HENGE du Côté d'Occident.

Vûe de STONE-HENGE du Côté du Midi.

21

PUTTING UP THE STONES
the fine art of levitating lintels

Fetching 50 tonne sarsen stones from the Marlborough Downs and 4 or 5 tonne bluestones from the Welsh Preseli mountains must have demanded a good working technology of ropes and levers, rollers and cradles.

The large stones were dressed on site, and rolled or dragged to a waiting hole-socket. A crane-like structure was probably used to pull them up to the vertical. Perhaps the 'Y' and 'Z' holes (*see plan on page 33*) held the props for this perilous process – for no stones were ever placed in them.

It is assumed, without a shred of evidence, that the lintels were raised by progressively adding to the height of a wooden cradle whilst levering up the lintel. Presumably the 7 tonne lintel was then perilously slid across to meet the awaiting tenons in the sarsen uprights. Do not try this at home! Is it unfeasible to suppose that an earth or timber ramp was constructed? Any other ideas?

The organisational skills required to complete the Sarsen circle, contemporary with the Great Pyramid, must make Stonehenge the eighth wonder of the ancient world.

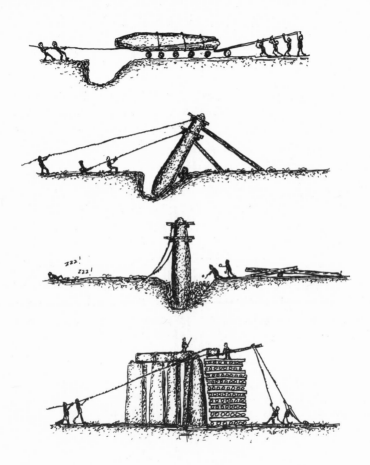

zzz!
zzz!

23

THE GHOST IN THE MACHINE
what is Stonehenge?

So just what have we got here on Salisbury Plain? Through all the *brouhaha*, speculation and confusion, is it possible to separate fact from fiction, theory from hard-won observation and proof? And how do we begin to assess any *spiritual sciences* that the site may amplify or resonate to? Scientists have not been able to do that ... yet!

Perhaps the best one can do is to recognise that Stonehenge was built by people identical to ourselves, albeit very different in culture yet perhaps superior in their ability to think about the fundamental issues concerning human life on earth.

In addition, the stones did not arrive or become placed by magic. The site was prepared, surveyed and marked out by people like us. Stones were transported, men and animals fed, equipment brought in and maintained.

And it must be true that *someone* was the architect of the various phases, and knew precisely *why* he or she was building *what* at that precise spot on Salisbury Plain. Taking the Thom survey plan (*next page*), how do we begin to understand what it may be telling us?

STONEHENGE COMPLETE
not just a load of old lintels

It was not until 1973 that an adequately accurate survey plan of Stonehenge was finally produced. It fell to Professor Alexander Thom and his family, assisted by Professor Richard Atkinson, to survey the site to an accuracy of half an inch (*shown opposite*).

The task in hand is how to reconstruct the 'service manual' for Stonehenge. The orientation to the midsummer sunrise was first spotted by William Stukeley whose 18th century engraving is shown on the previous page. The alignment was finally measured by theodolite in 1901 by the Astronomer Royal, Sir Norman Lockyer. The lunar astronomy was missed for a further fifty years, because our culture had previously failed to see the importance of the Moon in megalithic culture.

Early in 1963 'Peter' Newham, a retired gas-board manager, discovered a remarkable link between solar and lunar astronomy and the geometry of the station stones. The extreme solar and lunar positions fall at right angles to each other here. Only within half a degree of the latitude of Stonehenge can this occur (*see page 33*).

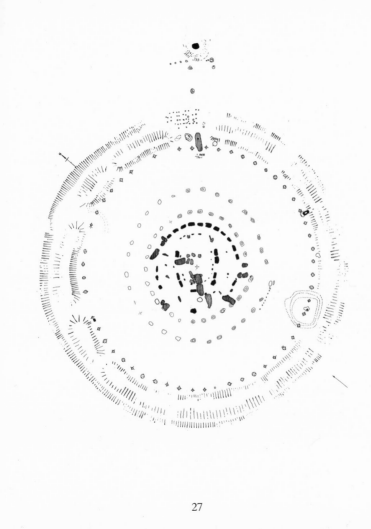

HERE COMES THE SUN
the 'midsummer' alignment

At the latitude of Stonehenge, the annual range of sunrises and sunsets each sweep angles of forty degrees either side of an east-west line. Thus the midsummer sunrise, shown opposite viewed from *outside* the sarsen circle through the towering giant trilithon, appears from a point on the horizon 50° east of north. The axis of the avenue very closely aligns to this, Alexander Thom measuring 49° 57'.

The commonly held belief that the sun rises over the heelstone at midsummer is actually wrong. All those beautiful images are a trick (or fabrication - *see opposite*), taken off axis; yet the Sun did actually rise from the axis of the avenue in neolithic times. However, these images reinforce the fact that Stonehenge is a temple aligned to the midsummer sunrise, and thus to the *seasonal* year of 365.242 days.

Because the earth's axial tilt has reduced by half a degree since Stonehenge was built, this 'heelstone rising' is more convincing now than in 2000 BC. In addition, the midwinter sunset lies *opposite* the midsummer sunrise and shines into Stonehenge from the south-west (*see too pages 39 and 43*).

WOODHENGE
another midsummer alignment

Just down the road, to the north-east of Stonehenge, may be found Woodhenge, a most interesting neolithic site. Dating from 2000 BC, archaeologists think it may have been a roofed building. Whatever Woodhenge once was, its axis is also accurately aligned to the midsummer sunrise.

The complex arrangement of postholes holds an interesting geometry, for Woodhenge is six concentric ellipsoids in plan, having perimeters of 40, 60, 80, 100, 140 and 160 Megalithic yards, the whole design based on a 12:35:37 right triangle of half MY units – and one wonders why.

Many megalithic sites have their entrances to a solstice sunrise or set. The most famous are Newgrange in Ireland, Bryn Celli-Ddu on Anglesey, Maes Howe in the Orkneys and, of course, Stonehenge. These are *ritual* alignments, often not terribly accurate yet connecting man with the skies and to the seasonal flow of time.

Some alignments are accurate to a *sixtieth* of a degree, occasionally marking the 18.62 year lunar cycle, particularly those sites thought to have been used to detect the tiny 'wobble' of the Moon, and thereby to predict eclipses.

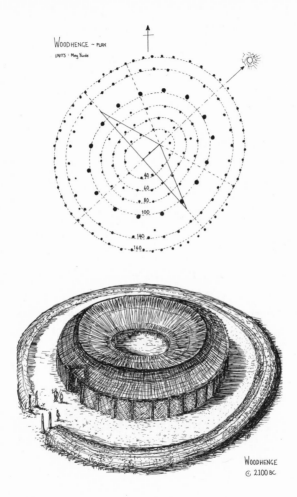

WOODHENGE ~ PLAN

UNITS : Meg Yards

40
60
80
100
140
160

WOODHENGE
ⓒ 2100 BC

31

CALENDAR CAPERS
the reasons for the seasons

Stonehenge is astronomically and geometrically locked into the cycles of the Sun and Moon. Even in the numbers of stones and their dimensional spacing one repeatedly finds the numbers of the solar year and lunar month. In the diagram opposite we find the 5:12 rectangle defining the eight key solar festivals of the year.

The Aubrey circle suggests a calendar of *thirteen* months of 28 days – a 364 day year. The thirty upright stones of the Sarsen circle suggest the Egyptian calendar of *twelve* months of thirty days – totalling 360 days. Twenty-nine uprights were full width and one was deliberately made half-width (*see page 19*), an attempt to represent in stone the $29\frac{1}{2}$ day lunation cycle (the time between two full moons). Twice $29\frac{1}{2}$ makes 59, the number of 'Y' and 'Z' holes and also the total number of stones in the bluestone circle.

The bluestone horseshoe contains nineteen stones. In exactly nineteen years there are almost exactly 235 lunations – the most perfect repeat cycle of the Sun and Moon.

235 divided by 19 is $12\frac{7}{19}$, the number of lunations (full moons) in one year. Seven nineteenths is 0.368.

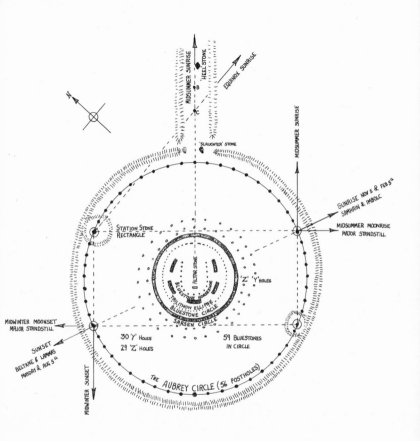

MIDSUMMER SUNRISE
'HEEL STONE'
EQUINOX SUNRISE
MIDSUMMER SUNRISE
'SLAUGHTER' STONE
SUNRISE NOV 5 & FEB 5th
SAMHAIN & IMBOLC
MIDSUMMER MOONRISE
MAJOR STANDSTILL
STATION STONE
RECTANGLE
'Z' 'Y' HOLES
ALTAR STONE
BLUESTONE HORSESHOE
TRILITHON ELLIPSE
BLUESTONE CIRCLE
SARSEN CIRCLE
MIDWINTER MOONSET
MAJOR STANDSTILL
SUNSET
BELTANE & LAMMAS
MAYDAY & AUG 5th
30 'Y' HOLES
29 'Z' HOLES
59 BLUESTONES
IN CIRCLE
MIDWINTER SUNSET
THE AUBREY CIRCLE (56 POSTHOLES)

THE LUNATION TRIANGLE
the marriage of the Sun and Moon

The secret of the calendar (and eclipse prediction) is to be able to find the exact number of lunations (full moons) in the solar year. On the previous page we showed this to be 12.368, almost exactly $12\frac{7}{19}$.

A clue to solving this calendrical conundrum can be found at the Station Stone rectangle (*see page 15*) or by a rope marked with 30 equal lengths. Peg out a 5:12:13 triangle, divide the '5' side into '3' and '2'. At the 3:2 point, a constructed hypotenuse to the apex has a length of $\sqrt{153}$, which is 12.369 units. Neat! The disciples catching 153 fishes in the net in the last chapter of St John's Gospel tantalisingly suggests continuity of cultural knowledge of the lunation triangle.

The plot now thickens – a Megalithic yard divides into a foot (12 inches) and an Egyptian Royal cubit (20.64 inches). If the Megalithic yard is taken as one lunation period, then where foot and cubit meet is found to be 0.368 lunations, thus 12 MY + 1 foot = 365.22 days, or one solar year!

Thus the measures of antiquity enshrine the secret of the calendar, and, not surprisingly, Stonehenge enshrines both.

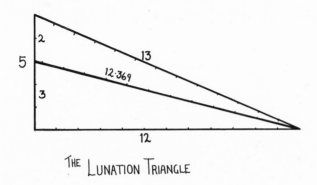

THE LUNATION TRIANGLE

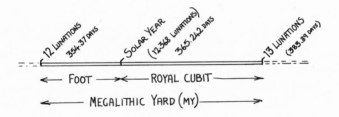

GEOMETRY, ASTRONOMY & METROLOGY MEET WITHIN THE STATION STONES

35

ROLLING STONES

long distance stone moving and a huge triangle

The Sarsen Stones were moved over 20 miles from the Fyfield Down, adjacent to Avebury. The smaller bluestones came originally from *Carn Meini* (*"dressed stone cairn"*) in the Preseli Mountains of West Wales. Some think they came by glacier, others that they were lugged to Milford Haven, then rafted. The large altar stone (*opposite top*) at Stonehenge is made from a sparkly sandstone found adjacent to the Haven; did a glacier transport it *uphill* to Salisbury Plain? Hardly, the Haven was never glaciated. Humans 1, Glaciers 0.

The latitudes of the bluestone and sarsen sites are precisely one seventh of 364° and 360° respectively. What *is* going on here – calendar magic?

Another Lunation Triangle (*shown opposite within a massive north-south-east-west 5:12 station stone rectangle scale 2500:1*) incorporates the location of Stonehenge, the bluestone site and completes a right angled triangle via Lundy Island and Caldey Island. In Old Welsh, Lundy is *Ynys Elen*, the 'island of the elbow, or right–angle'. Could this be the reason why Stonehenge is located *where* it is – as the only man–made construction in a geomantic message about calendar wisdom?

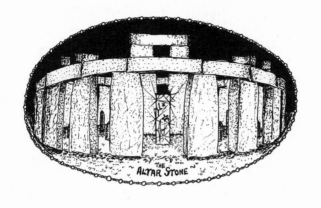

THE ALTAR STONE

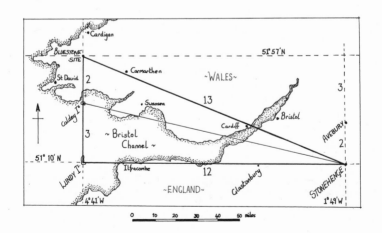

PREDICTING ECLIPSES

who nodes how it is done?

Anyone who has tried to make a model of how the Sun and Moon move around the sky will end up, most simply, with a circle of 28 markers around a central earth. Moving a 'Moon-Pole' one position per day and a 'Sun-Pole' once every 13 days, provides a calendar accurate to 98%.

Twice every year, for about 34 days, the full and new moons cross the Sun's apparent path in the sky (the ecliptic) and eclipses result. These two *eclipse seasons*, which are 173 days apart, move backwards around the calendar taking 18.6 years to complete a revolution. The two precise points where the Moon crosses the Sun's path are called the *lunar nodes*.

By doubling the sun-moon calendar to the 56 markers of the Aubrey circle (*shown opposite*), we can obtain an accuracy of 99.8%. Conveniently, 18.6 x 3 is almost 56 (or 28 x 2) and now the 3:2 ratio enables eclipses to be reliably predicted.

Why not build one of these at home, following the simple instructions opposite? Remember that a full or new Moon within the shaded eclipse zone predicts a lunar or solar eclipse. A lunar eclipse will always be visible at a given location if the Moon rises within the half hour before sunset.

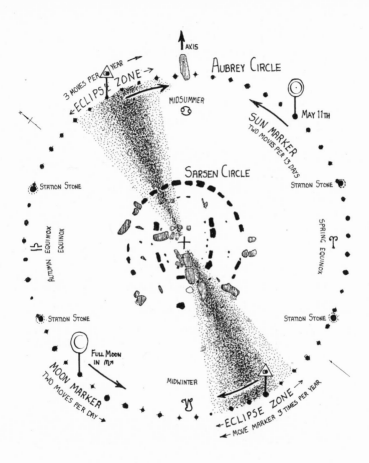

AXIS

3 MOVES PER YEAR →

← ECLIPSE ZONE →

MIDSUMMER

AUBREY CIRCLE

SUN MARKER
TWO MOVES PER 13 DAYS

MAY 11TH

STATION STONE

SARSEN CIRCLE

STATION STONE

SPRING EQUINOX

AUTUMN EQUINOX

EQUINOX

STATION STONE

STATION STONE

FULL MOON
IN ♏

MOON MARKER
TWO MOVES PER DAY →

MIDWINTER

♑

ECLIPSE ZONE →
← MOVE MARKER 3 TIMES PER YEAR

HOLES OF TIME
switching Stonehenge on again

Many visitors presently think the central stone construction (*see Stukeley's impression opposite*) is all there is to Stonehenge, and hardly notice the concrete-filled Aubrey holes as they step over them. But, as we have seen, these are numerically perfect for predicting eclipses, lunar phase and recording the solar and lunar positions, and the state of the sea-tides. The Greeks, in the 4th century BC, taught that the number 56 was connected with eclipses, dragons and demons.

It would not affect the monument one jot to have the Stonehenge calendar up and running as an educational aid. Imagine the job title - what long hours, lots of overtime!

The secret of the calendar, the extra $\frac{7}{19}$ of a lunation (*pages 32-37*) is enshrined as the relative sizes of the two main defining features at Stonehenge (*shown below*).

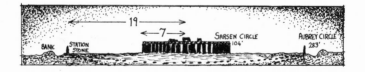

THE MIDDLE GROUND
the stones at the centre of the world

———————————

To walk inside the central area of Stonehenge today requires that the visitor applies for a 'special access' tour from the custodians, English Heritage. With nearly one million visitors a year, the monument is under increasing pressure from the sheer numbers of people who wish to wander amidst our national temple.

The plan shown opposite, of the central area enclosed by the sarsen circle, is from Edgar Barclay's 1895 book *Stonehenge and its Earthworks*. Apart from the fact that the fallen trilithon (stones 57, 58 and lintel 158) has since been re-erected (in 1958), this plan is similar to the Stonehenge we see today. The concentric solid lines indicate the bluestone horseshoe, bluestone circle and sarsen circle respectively.

The numbering system for the stones, as found opposite, remains to this day. Of particular interest is stone 11, the half-width sarsen upright, stone 150, a bluestone with mortise holes and stone 68, the grooved bluestone (*see page 15*).

Shown also is stone 156, the trilithon lintel curiously mortised on *both* sides, apparently erroneously. We might guess that this muddle engendered some megalithic swearing!

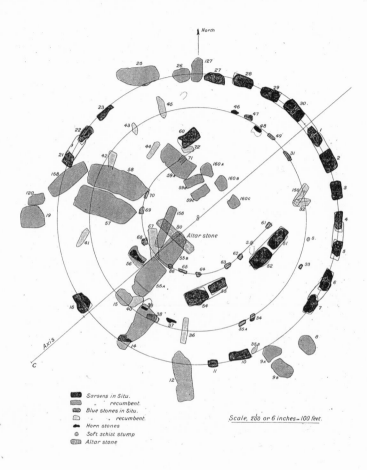

North

Axis

C

Sarsens in Situ.
"   "   recumbent.
Blue stones in Situ.
"   "   recumbent.
Horn stones
Soft schist stump
Altar stone

Scale, 200 or 6 inches = 100 feet.

SQUARING THE CIRCLE
the Moon and Earth show how it is done

Ever since Inigo Jones' hexagonal linking of the sarsen circle to the five trilithons (the King's architect thought there were six – *bottom left*) people have been attempting to fit the layout of Stonehenge to a meaningful geometric design. The most successful designs are shown opposite.

John Michell's most elegant solution to squaring the circle using the Earth and Moon (*top left*) also defines two circles of the inner sanctum of Stonehenge (*top right*). Michell's geometry also postulates a hexagonal solution to the placing of the bluestone circle within the sarsen circle. In a squared circle the perimeter of the square and circle are the same.

John Martineau's recent octagonal solution (*below right*) also masterfully accounts for the width of the stones in the bluestone horseshoe. His other octagonal solution is shown later on page 49.

Geometry is one practical method by which the megalithic builders could have linked the various phases of Stonehenge together. The seven-fold geometry linking the Aubrey circle to the sarsen circle (*see page 17*) is so precise as to confirm this technique.

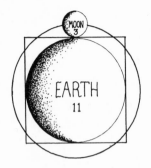

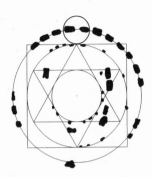

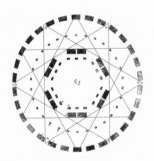

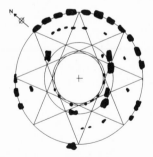

PYRAMIDAL CONNECTIONS
uncanny similarities

___

If it were possible to slice the earth in half, with the resulting Great Circle passing through *both* Stonehenge and the Great Pyramid, then many other ancient sacred sites would also share the same fate, including Mecca, Crete and Delphi. The circle would also run along the '13' side of the lunation triangle (*illustrated on page 37*) to the bluestone site.

Sir William Flinders-Petrie showed that the Great Pyramid was constructed using the Royal cubit of 1.72 feet. The connection with the foot and the MY is shown on page 35.

Silbury Hill, near Avebury, and the Great Pyramid reciprocate their respective latitudes and angles of slope (*shown below*). Such observations suggest cultural connections which do not fit our present model of the ancient world.

51°51'

THE GREAT PYRAMID
LATITUDE 30° N

30°

SILBURY HILL
LATITUDE 51° 24' N

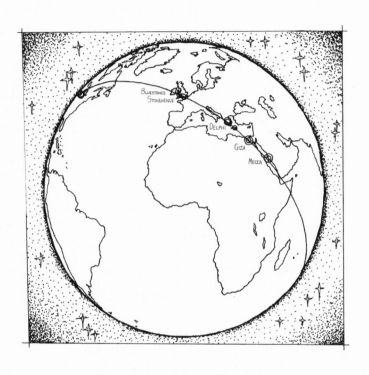

THE STONEHENGE-GIZA GREAT CIRCLE

THE OCTAGONAL EARTH
where seven meets eight

The Earth's tilt angle is about one eighth of a circle, varying between 21° and 24° over a 41,000 year cycle. This tilt defines the tropics of Cancer and Capricorn and the Arctic and Antarctic circles. A cross-section through the poles reveals an broadly octagonal earth, just as the solstices, equinoxes and 'quarter' days define an octagonal year.

In John Martineau's diagram opposite, we see the heelstone creating an octagram which precisely defines the diameter of the Aubrey circle, the positions of the four station stones and also neatly frames the sarsen circle.

The octagonal geometry of Stonehenge thus mimics that of the Earth in space. Earlier we showed the strong sevenfold geometry (perhaps based on the Sun, Moon and five visible planets) between Aubrey and sarsen circles, and how sevenness is invoked by both the latitude of Stonehenge and the midsummer sunrise angle (*pages 16-17*).

Seven and eight thus form important number signatures for the monument and, interestingly, produce 56 when multiplied - the number of Aubrey holes.

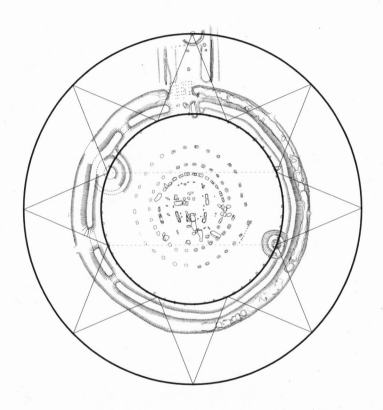

TRAVELS TO THE OTHERWORLD
a culture of life after death

The Stonehenge landscape includes many examples of what are known as barrows (*opposite*). There are many types, some containing burials or cremated remains. The artefacts buried with the dead provide archaeologists with much information about the Wessex Culture. The foetal position of many burials suggests a rebirth from within Mother Earth. That burial chambers are often aligned to the midwinter Sun suggests a similar symbolism, with the 'death' of the Sun at its lowest point in the sky, from which it then always rises.

An excavation at Stonehenge recently unearthed the body of an archer, with arrowheads still lodged in his vertebrae. Ritual sacrifice, execution or murder? We will never know.

1. LONG BARROW.

3. BELL BARROW.   2. BOWL BARROW.

4. DRUID BARROW.

51

BARROWLOADS OF GOLD
a ninefold astronomical lozenge

At the early Bronze Age Bush Barrow, just north of Stonehenge, Stukeley found nothing, whilst Cunningham, in 1808, plundered his finest treasure - the Bush Barrow *lozenge*.

Lying over the breast of a once tall man this exquisite lozenge made from beaten gold was once mounted on a wooden plate and measures 7 inches in length. Bronze rivets, mixed with wood and thin strips of bronze were interred nearby. It may be seen today in Devizes museum.

The internal angles of the lozenge are 80° and 100° and this reflects a strong nine-fold geometry, whilst each side possesses nine triangles and the central diamond has nine inner diamonds. The sharp ends of the lozenge have the same angle as the range of sunrises and sunsets at the latitude of Stonehenge - was it a sighting device? The wider angles take care of the extreme lunar rises and sets.

Our man was also buried with two metal daggers, a bronze axe, a lance-head, a second gold lozenge, a gold belt-hook, a stone mace-head and decorated bone ornaments. In fact, not at all the normal tackle of a modern astronomer.

STAR CULTURE
before Stonehenge

Before Stonehenge and the start of Neolithic culture, the people of southern Britain built *longbarrows* – long multiple chambered burial chambers. Examples open to the public include Belas Knap and West Kennett, Avebury (*opposite*). These enigmatic structures, like giant's sleeping bags, were often aligned to important risings and settings of stars. The diagram below (*after Thom*), shows the setting points of major fixed stars on the western horizon in 2000 BC.

Stukeley's curious diagram of the Stonehenge Avenue is shown (*opposite below*). 1800 feet in length, this major feature of the monument is barely visible today. Perhaps it was a processional walkway to the monument in a time when star ritual assumed numinous importance to the culture.

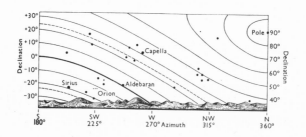

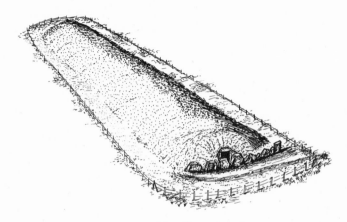

~ WEST KENNET LONG BARROW ~

INSPIRATIONAL STONEHENGE
a source of wonder and amazement

Stonehenge may elude us, but it also inspires us. The monument taunts our smallness, yet celebrates our abilities. Our culture assumes superiority whilst those stones point to things we have forgotten, and they mock our *hubris* in so doing. We might humbly remember the words of the poet Drayton, who, in *Polyalbion*, wrote:

> *"Ill did those mighty men to trust thee with their story,*
> *Thou hast forgot their names, who raised thee for their glory."*

Stonehenge has inspired many fine artists throughout history – Constable, Turner, Blake and Henry Moore all worked with the monument, together with melodramatic lesser artists (*see opposite*). Poets and writers have also dipped their pens into the dark ink of those 'immemorial grey pillars'.

Perhaps, like the black monolith in Arthur C. Clarke's *2001, A Space Odyssey*, Stonehenge begins a process of increased consciousness, most notably of the true rhythms of human life and the cycles of the Sun and Moon. We moderns have lost most of that, and need with some urgency to reclaim our long-lost heritage from Stonehenge.

"It's true Edgar, the solstice was yesterday!"

Further reading

"The Stonehenge People" &
"A Field Guide to the Stone Circles of Britain, Ireland & Brittany"
by Dr. Aubrey Burl,

"Stonehenge" by Prof. Richard Atkinson,

"Stonehenge, Mysteries of the Stones & Landscape" by David Souden,

"Sun, Moon & Stonehenge" & *"Sun, Moon & Earth"*
by Robin Heath.

STONEHENGE, AS IT WAS AND AS IT IS.
THE ENCLOSURE OF THE ANCIENT MONUMENT.